The Man Who
The Five Dogs

By Cynthia-Mae Hunt
Illustrated by Grisel Montes

The Man Who Walks
The Five Dogs

By Cynthia-Mae Hunt
Illustrated by Grisel Montes

The stories and images in this book are true and are written based on the perceptive description shared from my father's experiences during his walks.

Prelude

This book is dedicated to my dad, "The Man Who Walks The Five Dogs." I admire him for his dedication to maintain a healthy lifestyle living with multiple sclerosis. He has taught me about having compassion for others by simply waving a 'stick' every day when he walks the family of five little puppies.

This book features anecdotes of his stories he has shared with me and my mother when he returns home from his walks with the puppies.

Thank You

To Mommy: I would like to thank you for your constant support, doting, and for always pushing me to be my best!

To Mr. & Mrs. Copeland: I would like to thank you for helping me brand the idea to write this book.

To Auntie Grisel & Uncle Ray: I would like to thank you for helping me illustrate my ideas and make them come to life.

Lastly, I would like to thank everyone who shares smiles, and acts of kindness with my dad and the puppies on their daily walks.

TABLE OF CONTENTS

10 Miles A Day

There is a man who lives in the City of Greensboro in North Carolina. This man has five little puppies.

Sir John wears a red collar, Duchess Robyn wears a pink collar, Duke Turner wears a green collar, Prince George wears a blue collar, and Princess Charlotte wears a purple collar.

Sir John and Duchess Robyn are married...

and, their three adorable children are Duke Turner, Prince George and Princess Charlotte.

The man walks the puppies three times a day. He walks the puppies at 6:00 AM so they can watch the sun rise and start their day.

The man and the puppies always try to walk between 15,000 and 20,000 steps a day.

He walks the puppies once at noon so they can get some fresh air.

The man then walks the puppies once between 5 PM and 8 PM so they can enjoy the cool air and see the sun set.

The man feeds the puppies twice a day.

The man loves to feed the puppies dog food with chicken, and rice, and all kinds of yummy things in it...

once at 8 AM and again at 8 PM.

After the puppies' evening walk, they get tummy rubs...

they have their faces cleaned for five minutes...

and, the man says goodnight to the puppies and they say goodnight to the world and go to sleep.

zzzzz

6 AM Walk

The man loves living in Greensboro even though it can get really hot there. To prevent the puppies from getting sick, the man gets up very early to take the puppies on their 6 AM walk.

This helps the puppies since they're Shih Tzus.

If the puppies are walked when it's hot, they can have trouble breathing, be tired from the heat, become sick from not having enough water, or even catch an infection.

The puppies enjoy watching the sun come up during their 6 AM walk as they trot down the sidewalk with their tails raised high.

After the 6 AM walk, the puppies eat their breakfast. The 6 AM walk always makes the puppies very sleepy.

The puppies like to take a nap every day after they finish their breakfast to have energy to play later.

A Treat For The Day

After Duchess Robyn had the puppies, things changed. Robyn didn't want to eat dog food anymore.

The man thought to himself, 'I love chicken and I know the dogs will, too and rotisserie chicken seems like it would be the easiest kind of chicken to find in stores.'

So, the man started giving Duchess Robyn and Sir John chicken once in a while as a treat. The man started giving their children chicken when they got older.

When the man brings chicken into the house the puppies, especially Robyn, open their eyes really wide and start wagging their tails.

The man cuts up the chicken and tries to take off as much skin as he can because skin is bad for the puppies. The man wants the puppies to only eat pure meat.

The man then puts the chicken into five bowls in separate spots.

The puppies love chicken and make the man very happy by eating every last bite!

The Umbrella

One day, the man was walking with the puppies. He was walking back to his home from Jesse Wharton Elementary School on Lake Brandt Road when the sky opened up. He felt a drop of water, and another, and another until the drops came again and again. The man began to walk faster. He did not like when he or the puppies got wet.

Suddenly, a car stopped near the man and the driver rolled down the window. The man inside the car said, "Hey, it's raining, and we see you walking all the time. Here's an umbrella," the man in the car said while giving an umbrella to the man with the puppies.

"Oh, thank you!" the man who walks the five dogs said. The car sped away and the man and the puppies began walking again. The man was very happy and surprised that someone gave him an umbrella.

He kept walking home thinking to himself, 'Man, people in Greensboro are nice!'

The Walking Stick

One nice and sunny morning, the man and the puppies were walking down Lake Brandt Road. They were near a neighborhood called North Beech, when suddenly a very happy lady came running out of that neighborhood. She began running after the man walking the puppies.

She shouted out to the man making him and the puppies look her way. The puppies looked at the lady without barking. The lady said to the man, "I made you a walking stick to protect you from animals or stray dogs."

The lady passed the man a big stick
that had spirals shaped into it near
the top that went round, and round
leaving the bottom
half of the stick
straight. The lady
then smiled
at the man
and the
puppies...

NORTH BEECH

and then walked back to North Beech.

The man and the puppies began walking home with the golden rays of sunshine, shining down on them to prepare for their next adventure in the city they love called Greensboro.

Made in the USA
Columbia, SC
06 June 2019